51 things to make with
Paper Plates

Fiona Hayes

Contents

Basic Equipment

Most of these projects use some or all of the following equipment, so keep these handy:

- **White glue**
- **Scissors**
- **Pencils**
- **Ruler**
- **Felt-tip pens**
- **Paintbrushes**

Large paper plates and small paper bowls are used unless otherwise stated.

Dotted Frog

What is spotted, dotted, and goes hoppity, hoppity? A little green frog, of course!

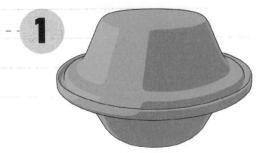

1 Glue two paper bowls together and paint them green.

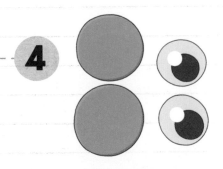

2 Cut off a section from a toilet tube and glue to the bowls, as shown. Paint the toilet tube green.

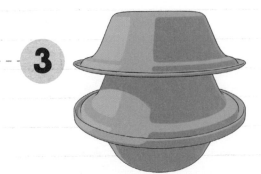

3 Paint another bowl green. Place it on top of the toilet tube and glue it into position.

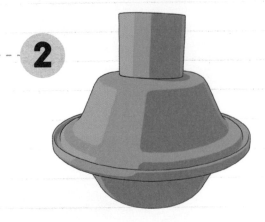

4 Cut two circles from the cardstock. They should be slightly larger than the googly eyes. Paint them green. Glue the eyes to the circles.

5

Cut two triangles from a small paper plate, for the frog's feet. Paint the triangles green.

6

Glue the eyes and feet in place. Paint the frog's belly pale green.

7

Add some dots to decorate your frog. Then make your frog hoppity-hop away!

RIBBET

RIBBET

Handy Hint

Let your paint dry completely before gluing the pieces together.

Snappy Crab

Who knew you could make a crab from paper plates? Your friends will want to SNAP up this seaside wonder when they see it!

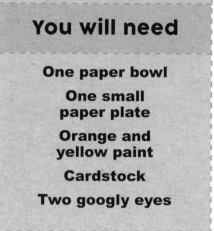

1

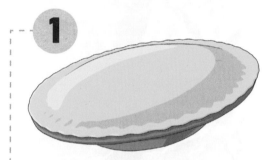

Paint a paper bowl orange. Paint a paper plate yellow. Glue the plate to the top of the bowl.

2

Cut out six legs from cardstock and paint orange. Bend them to look like a Z, as shown.

3

Glue the legs to the yellow paper plate.

4

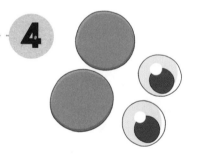

Cut out two circles from cardstock. They should be slightly larger than the googly eyes. Paint them orange. Glue the eyes to the circles.

5

Cut out two claws from cardstock and paint them orange.

6

Turn your crab over so that the bowl is at the top. Bend the bottoms of the cardstock circles and glue the eyes and claws in place.

7

Add some spots to finish your crab, but watch out for those snapping claws!

SNAP
SNAP

Butterfly Garland

This pretty bunting will brighten up any room in your home. Why not hang it in your bedroom?

1

To make one butterfly, fold a paper plate in half and cut out sections, as shown.

2

Unfold the plate. Next, paint it a bright color. You could decorate it with spots, too.

3

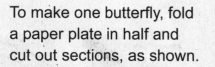

Glue two bendy straws for the body and antennae. Repeat the steps to make three more butterflies.

4

Glue a long length of ribbon to the backs of the butterflies to join them together.

5

Hang the butterfly bunting in your room to make a pretty decoration.

Christmas Tree Garland

Bring some festive cheer into your home with this colorful garland.

You will need

One paper plate
Paint, including green
Brown cardstock
Ribbon

1 Cut a paper plate into six sections.

2 Paint the sections green. Paint on lots of baubles.

3 Cut strips of brown cardstock for the trunks and glue them to the backs of the trees.

4 Glue a long piece of ribbon to the backs of the trees to join them together.

5 Hang your garland in a window to make a festive decoration.

9

Owl Mask

If you like wearing disguises, you'll love making this amazing owl mask—hoot, hoot, guess who!

You will need

Two paper plates
Paint, including yellow
Cardboard
Elastic

1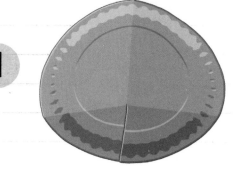

Paint a paper plate purple and fold it in half. Unfold the plate and make a slit along the fold line a third of the way up.

2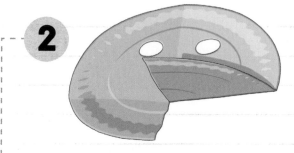

Use the end of a pencil to make a hole for your scissors, then cut out two holes for the eyes.

3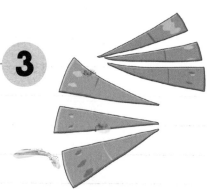

Cut out some feathers from another plate. Paint them purple.

4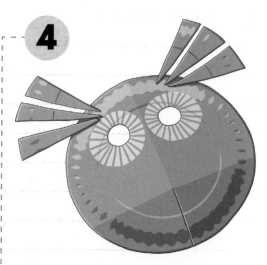

Paint some contrasting colored circles around the eyes and add extra detail. Glue the feathers to either side of the face.

5

Fold the bottom
of the cut end
inward so the pieces overlap, as
shown. Glue them to hold in place.

6

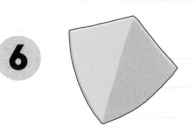

Cut out a beak from cardboard
and paint yellow. Fold it in half
to give it a crease.

7

Glue the beak in place. Attach a
piece of elastic from one side of
the mask to the other side
to finish your owl mask.

HOOT
HOOT

Panda

Pandas love to eat bamboo!
Can you make some to feed
your hungry bear?

You will need

Cardboard
One paper plate
Two paper bowls
Black and white paint
Green cardstock
Pink felt
Two googly eyes

1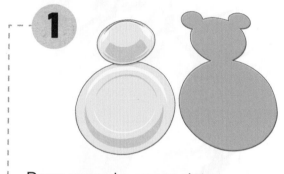

Draw around a paper plate
and a paper bowl onto a piece
of cardboard. Add ears, as shown.
Now cut out the shape.

2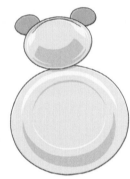

Glue the plate
and bowl to the
cardstock shape.

3

Glue another
bowl upside-
down to the
plate, to make
the panda's tummy.

4

Paint the top half of the body
black. Give the panda black
ears and a pair of big black
blotches around the eyes.

5

Cut out pairs of
legs and arms
from cardboard.
Paint them black.

6 Glue the arms and legs to the back of the body.

7 Gently bend the panda's legs forward so it can sit.

8 Cut out some circles of green cardstock. Glue the eyes to these circles and then glue them onto the face. Cut out a nose from pink felt and glue it on. Draw on a mouth to finish your panda.

Handy Hint
Make your panda some bamboo from straws and cardstock.

Peacock

You'll be proud as a peacock when you have made this pretty bird!

You will need

Three paper plates

Paint, including turquoise and yellow

Yellow and purple cardstock

Two googly eyes

1

Fold a paper plate as shown. Glue to hold in place. The folds will be at the back of the peacock.

2

Cut the bottom off another plate. Paint both plates turquoise.

3

Cut a third plate into sections, as shown. Paint them a darker shade of turquoise.

4

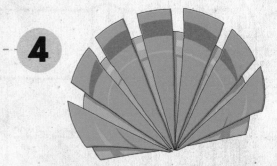

Fan out the plate sections. Glue them to the plate with the flat base. This is the peacock's tail.

5

Glue the folded plate to the tail.

6

Cut out a semi-circle for the peacock's feet from the yellow cardstock. Cut out a diamond for the beak.

7

Glue the yellow feet to the back of the body. Then glue the beak in place. Cut out some circles of purple cardstock (slightly bigger than the googly eyes). Glue the eyes to the cardstock and then glue in place.

8

Cut out some circles from yellow cardstock and paint on some different colored details.

9

Glue the circles to your peacock's tail feathers to finish it off.

Handy Hint

Use clothespins to hold pieces in place while waiting for them to dry.

Robot

Join the robot revolution by making this cool robot!

You will need

Three paper bowls
Two paper plates
One long cardboard tube
Corrugated cardstock

Paint
Two jar lids
Shiny cardstock
Felt
Two googly eyes

1

Glue two paper bowls together to make the body. Paint them a dark color.

2

Glue a paper plate to the top of another bowl and paint another color. This is the robot's head.

3

Glue the head to the body and leave to dry.

4

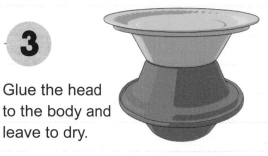

Cut two sections from the cardboard tube to make the legs. Cover with corrugated cardstock and paint.

5

Glue the legs to the bottom of the body.

6

Cut two sections from the edges of another paper plate and paint them. These are the arms.

7

Glue the arms to the body. Glue the two jar lids to the base of the legs. If you do not have any lids, use two circles of cardstock instead.

8

Cut out two U shapes from shiny cardstock. Then glue them to the arms. Cut out some circles of felt (slightly bigger than the googly eyes). Glue the eyes to the felt.

9

Glue the eyes to the head. Cut out a strip from corrugated cardstock to make a mouth and glue it on. Cut out some shiny circles to decorate your robot. Beep! Beep! Your robot is ready for action.

COOL

Seahorse

Shy and sweet, seahorses are one of the wonders of the seven seas. Why not decorate your house with this underwater beauty?

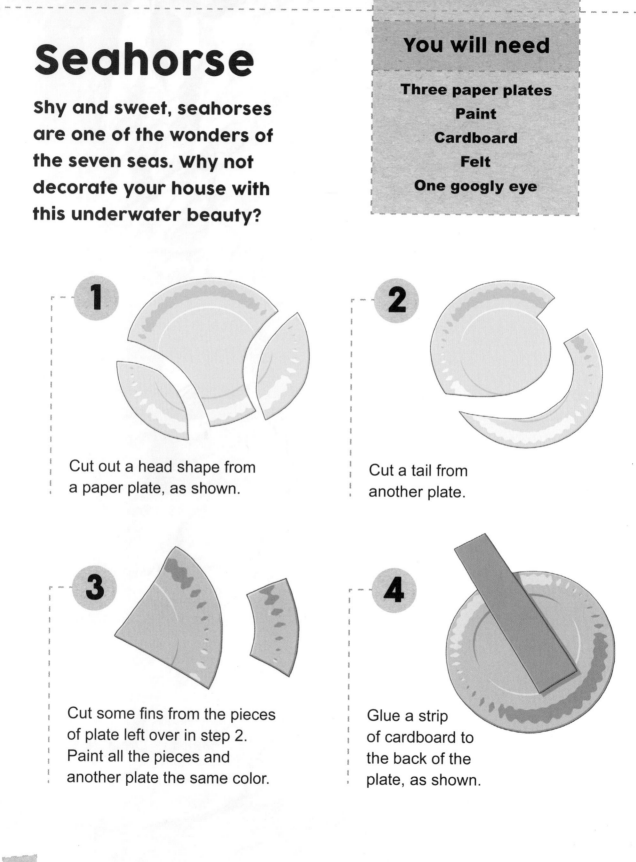

1 Cut out a head shape from a paper plate, as shown.

2 Cut a tail from another plate.

3 Cut some fins from the pieces of plate left over in step 2. Paint all the pieces and another plate the same color.

4 Glue a strip of cardboard to the back of the plate, as shown.

5

Glue the head to the cardboard strip.

6

Glue the tail and fins in place.

7

Cut out a circle from felt just bigger than the eye and glue the eye to it. Glue this onto the face. Paint on spots and stripes. Now your seahorse can swim away!

Handy Hint

Make the jellyfish on page 28 so that your seahorse has a friend to swim with!

Spotted Tortoise

Making this super-cute tortoise is so much fun you'll want to make a whole set of them!

You will need

One paper bowl

One paper plate

One long cardboard tube

One foam ball

Paint, including dark and light green

Purple felt

Googly eyes

1

Paint a paper bowl dark green and a paper plate light green. Glue the plate to the top of the bowl.

2

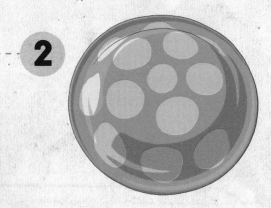

Turn the plate over so that the bowl is at the top. Paint large spots all over the bowl.

3

Cut four equal sections from a cardboard tube. Paint them to make the tortoise's legs.

4

Glue the legs to the plate, as shown.

5

Paint a foam ball and glue it to the front of the shell.

6

Cut out some circles of felt (slightly bigger than the googly eyes) and glue the eyes to them. Add to the ball. Add a smile to complete your spotted friend!

Handy Hint
Let the green paint dry completely before adding the spots.

Mouse Ears

Bring some magic into your dressing-up fun with these fabulous, fantastic ears!

You will need

One paper plate
Gray and pink paint
White cardstock

1

Paint a paper plate gray and cut out the center, as shown.

2

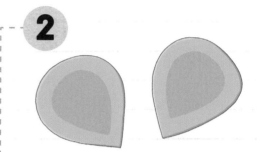

Cut out a large pair of ears from cardstock. Paint gray with a pink middle.

3

Glue the ears to the back of the plate.

4

Squeak, squeak! Your ears are ready to wear.

Fairy Toadstool

Make this fun toadstool for little fairies!

You will need

One paper bowl

Red, white, yellow, and blue paint

One paper cup

1 Paint a paper bowl red. When dry, add some white spots.

2 Paint a paper cup yellow. Cut out a doorway, as shown.

3 Glue the bowl to the cup.

4 Paint on some windows. Leave your toadstool on a window ledge so fairies can visit!

Wise Owl

This bright and colorful owl makes a perfect nighttime friend. Hoot, hoot!

You will need

One large paper plate

Cardboard

Two small paper plates

Two paper bowls

Purple, lilac, turquoise, and yellow paint

Purple and yellow cardstock

Two googly eyes

1

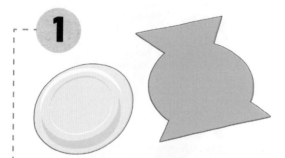

Draw around the large paper plate onto a thick piece of cardstock. Add shape to the top and bottom, as shown. Then cut out.

2

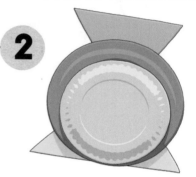

Paint the large plate purple and glue it onto the cardstock. Paint one small plate lilac and glue it onto the large plate. Paint the extra bit of cardstock at the bottom yellow to make the owl's feet.

3

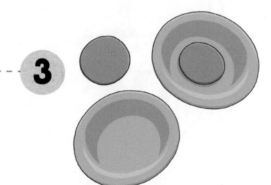

Paint the insides of two bowls turquoise. Cut out two circles of purple cardstock and glue one to the center of each bowl.

4

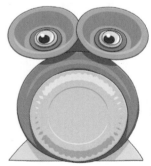

Glue both bowls to the top part of your cardstock shape. Cut out two circles from the yellow cardstock (slightly bigger than the googly eyes). Glue the eyes to the cardstock and then glue onto the purple circles.

5

Paint the second small plate purple, and then cut the plate in half.

6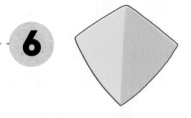

Cut a diamond shape from yellow cardstock for the beak.

7

Glue the wings and beak in place. Add some details to finish. Why not stick your wise owl onto your bedroom door?

HOOT
HOOT

Elephant

It's time for a craft safari. Step into the wild and make this adorable baby elephant.

You will need

Two paper plates
One paper bowl
Gray, pink, white, and purple paint
Cardstock
One googly eye

1

Paint one paper plate and the bowl gray.

2

Glue the bowl to the plate, as shown.

3

Cut out a trunk from the edge of a plate and an ear from the cardstock. Paint them gray. Then paint the middle of the ear pink.

4

Glue the ear and the trunk onto the elephant's body.

5

Cut out a pair of feet from the cardstock and paint them gray.

6

Glue the feet in place and paint on some toenails with white paint.

7

Cut out a tusk, a tail, and a circle just bigger than the googly eye from the cardstock. Paint the tusk white, the tail gray, and the circle purple. Glue them all into place, along with the googly eye, as shown. Why not make a herd of elephants for a safari adventure?

Handy Hint

Always wash and dry your paintbrushes after use.

Jellyfish

This pink sea creature will look great hanging in your room.

1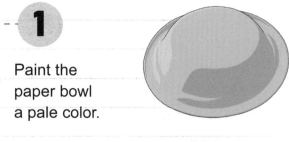

Paint the paper bowl a pale color.

2

When dry, paint on different colored spots. Make some of them overlap.

3

Glue on a pair of googly eyes.

4

Cut different lengths of curly gift ribbon. Tie them together at one end and tape them to the underside of the jellyfish.

5

Tape a length of elastic to the top of the bowl. Gently tug on it to watch your jellyfish bounce up and down.

Mice

Make these
marvelous mice!

You will need

One paper plate   Googly eyes

Gray, pink,
black, and
white paint

Cardstock

Pink felt

1

Cut the paper plate in half.
Set one half aside for later.

2

Make one half
of the plate into
a cone shape by folding the
two points of the semicircle
into the center. Glue it in place
and paint the cone gray.

3

Cut out some
ears from cardstock
and paint them gray.
Add some pink in the middle.

4

Cut a tapered
strip of pink felt
and glue it
on as a tail.
Glue the
ears in place.

5

Paint on a black
nose and some
spots. Add a pair
of googly eyes.

SQUEAK

29

Bunch of Flowers

1 Paint five paper bowls different bright colors.

2 Now cut eight evenly spaced slits from the curved edge to the flat center of three of the bowls. Shape the ends of the sections to look like petals.

3 Make the remaining bowls into daisies by cutting slits all the way around each bowl.

4 Scrunch up some small pieces of tissue paper and glue them to the center of each flower.

5 Cut some strips of cardboard and paint green. Glue to the back of your flowers for stems. Why not give your flowers to a friend or put them in a vase in your room?

Princess Tiara

You'll look pretty as a princess in this tiara.

You will need

Paper plate
Paint, including yellow
Cardstock
Glitter

1 Cut a paper plate into a C shape, as shown. Paint it bright yellow.

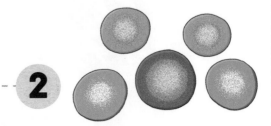

2 Cut out about five circles from the cardstock. Use paint and glitter to make them look like sparkling jewels.

3 Glue the jewels to the top of the tiara.

4 Finally, add some more detail so your tiara is fit for a princess. Do not forget to practice your royal wave!

Hippo

This hippo looks so happy he will have you grinning from ear-to-ear too!

You will need

One paper plate

Two paper bowls

Cardboard

White cardstock

Purple, dark pink, light pink, and green paint

Googly eyes

1 Cut one of the bowls in half. Paint the half bowl, a whole bowl, and a plate purple.

2 Paint the inside of the half bowl and bottom of the whole bowl dark pink, as shown. This will be the hippo's mouth.

3 Glue the half bowl to the whole bowl so that it looks like an open mouth.

4 Cut out a pair of ears and a pair of feet from cardboard. Paint them purple.

5

Glue the ears to the head, and then glue the head and feet to the large plate.

6

Cut out some teeth from white cardstock and glue them to the inside of the hippo's mouth.

7

Paint on some spots, nostrils, toenails, and the inside of the ears. Cut out two circles (slightly bigger than the googly eyes). Paint them green, glue on the eyes, and fix onto the head. Your hippo is ready to squelch through mud!

Handy Hint

The colored circles will make your hippo's eyes really stand out.

Chickens

Cluck, cluck! Time to make some cheerful chickens—are you ready?

You will need

One small paper plate

Two paper plates

Brown, yellow, gray, and white paint

Cardboard

Red cardstock

Four googly eyes

1 Cut a small paper plate in half. Set one half aside for the next chicken. Fold one piece in half and glue to hold together. Paint brown. This will be the chicken's tail.

2 Paint a plate brown and cut a small slit into one side, as shown. Cut out two triangles from cardboard and paint yellow, for the feet. Glue the feet to the back of the plate at mirrored points across the circle.

3 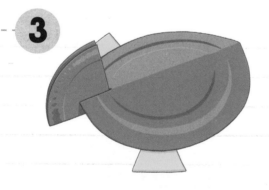 Fold the plate in half to make a crease. Unfold and slide the tail into the slit. Glue to hold in place.

4 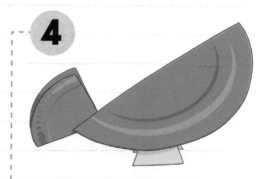 Refold the plate and glue to hold it in place.

5

Cut out two hearts from red cardstock to make a wattle and comb.

6

Cut out a triangle from cardboard and paint yellow, for the beak. Glue the beak, wattle, and comb in place.

7

Add a pair of googly eyes and some spots to finish your cheerful chicken.

Handy Hint

Place the feet in different positions to give your chicken different poses.

CLUCK
CLUCK

Penguin

Penguins are one of the cutest creatures on land—and sea! These birds are super-fast swimmers.

You will need

One paper plate
One white paper bowl
Yellow, black, and green paint
Cardboard
Two googly eyes

1

Fold down two flaps on a paper plate, as shown, and glue in position. Turn over, and paint the front black.

2

Glue a bowl to the front of the plate.

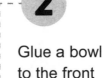

3

From cardboard, cut out a semi-circle for the penguin's feet and a diamond shape for its beak. Paint yellow.

4

Glue the feet to the back of the body.

5

Cut out some circles and paint them green. Glue the googly eyes to the circles, then glue the beak and eyes in place. Decorate your bathroom with the penguin, but, be warned— penguins love to swim!

Snail

Make two little snails and have a snail race!

1

Fold a paper plate in half. Glue to hold in place and paint a pale color.

2

Paint two paper bowls a darker color. Glue the bowls to either side of the folded plate, to make a shell.

3

Cut two circles from the cardstock and paint them. Glue the eyes to the circles, and glue onto the body. Cut two pieces of straw and glue them into place for horns.

4

Paint some more detail onto the shell. Your snail is ready to race away...slowly!

Alien

1 Glue two bowls together and paint bright yellow.

2 When dry, paint on pink spots.

3 Cut the edge off a paper plate into six sections, as shown, and paint yellow.

4 Fold a tab at the ends and glue the four long sections to the top bowl.

5 Add the last two pieces of plate edge as feet. Cut circles from the cardstock and paint them pink. Glue the eyes to the circles and then glue the circles to the stems. Paint on a squiggly mouth.

UFO

Is there anybody out there?
Make a spaceship and find out!

You will need

Two paper plates
One paper bowl
Dark and light blue paint
Cardstock
Shiny paper

1 Glue two large paper plates together and paint them dark blue.

2

Paint a small bowl light blue and glue it to the top of the plates.

3

Cut some windows from cardstock, draw on lots of aliens. Glue the windows to the small bowl on the UFO.

4

Add some shiny paper circles to the top plate. Tape some thread to the top of your UFO to hang it in the air. Your UFO is ready to beam back to Mars—but be careful that it doesn't take you with it!

Flower Picture Frame

You will need

One paper plate

Paint, including yellow

Cardstock

1

Use a pencil tip to make a hole in the paper plate for your scissors. Cut out the middle and paint the ring yellow.

2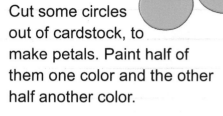

Cut some circles out of cardstock, to make petals. Paint half of them one color and the other half another color.

3

Glue the petals, alternating colors, to the back of the plate.

4

Continue until you have a circle of petals.

5

Cut out a cardstock circle, slightly larger than the hole in the flower. Add glue to half of the cardstock and attach to the back of the flower—so you can slide in your picture.

6

Decorate your frame and slide in your picture. You could use a photograph of yourself and give it to someone as a gift.

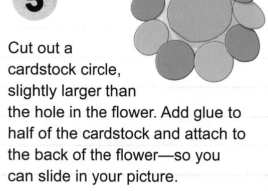

Fish

Swim with the fishes and decorate your bedroom with creatures from the sea.

You will need

Three paper plates

Light and dark orange and pink paint

Two googly eyes

1

Cut a slit in two paper plates, as shown, and fold back the slits to make a mouth.

2

Cut out a tail and two fins from another plate.

3

Paint all the pieces orange and the inside of the mouth pink. Add scales and dark orange circles for the eyes.

4

Glue the two plates together, with the tail trapped between them. Add the fins to either side of the body, and a pair of googly eyes.

41

Flower Hat

You'll look great in this pretty flower hat!

1 Use a pencil tip to make a hole for your scissors and cut out the middle of a paper plate.

2 Recycle the middle of the plate, but keep the ring. The ring should fit over the paper bowl.

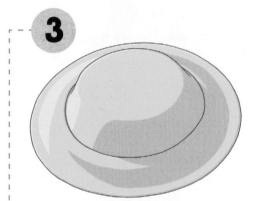

3 Place the ring over the paper bowl. Glue to hold in place. Paint your hat yellow.

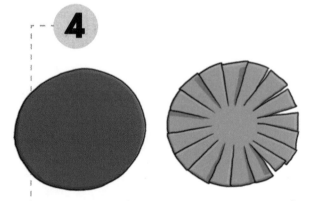

4 Cut out lots of small circles from colored cardstock. These will be flowers. Cut the edges, as shown, to make petals.

5

Glue the flowers around your hat.

6

Glue some balls of tissue paper into the centers of the flowers. Tie a big bow of ribbon and glue it to your hat. Now your hat is ready!

CUTE

Stegosaurus

This large, armored dinosaur is a plant-eating friendly giant! Can you make any more dinos?

1 For the body, cut the bottom off a paper plate and paint it.

2 Cut out a head, tail, and a pair of legs from cardboard. Paint them a contrasting color to the body.

3 Glue the head, tail, and legs to the back of the plate.

4 Cut out some triangles from cardboard and paint them. Glue them along the top of the body.

5 Paint on lots of spots, including one for the eye, and a mouth. Glue on a googly eye. Your dinosaur is ready to stomp!

Whale

1
Paint two paper plates blue.

2
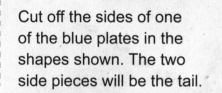

Cut off the sides of one of the blue plates in the shapes shown. The two side pieces will be the tail.

3
Cut out a curved piece of cardstock and paint blue.

4
Glue all the pieces together, as shown.

5
Paint on some spots, including a larger pink one for the eye, and a smile. Add a googly eye to bring your whale to life!

Bug Hat

Is it a bug? Is it a hat? It's both —and it will look great on you!

You will need

One paper bowl
Red and black paint
Two googly eyes
Black and yellow felt
Elastic

1 Paint the outside of a paper bowl red.

2 Paint on a black head and some spots.

3 To make legs, cut six strips of black felt and glue them to the body, as shown.

4 Attach a piece of elastic from one side of the bowl to the other.

5 Cut out some circles of felt (slightly bigger than the googly eyes) and glue the eyes to them. Glue to the bug. Why not repeat the steps to make different types of bugs?

Necklace

You will need

One paper plate
Yellow paint
Shiny paper

1

Cut the middle out of a paper plate. Keep the ring but recycle the rest.

2

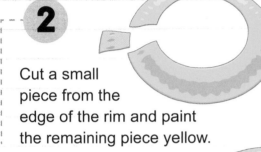

Cut a small piece from the edge of the rim and paint the remaining piece yellow.

3

Cut out lots of strips of shiny paper.

4

Glue the shiny paper around the necklace.

5

Add some extra detail and your necklace is ready. You could wear your necklace with the tiara from page 31—just like a real princess!

Dragon

1 Glue a strip of cardboard to the top edges of a small and large bowl.

2 Glue another small and another large bowl onto the top.

3 Cut out a crescent shape from the edge of a large plate. This will be the tail.

4 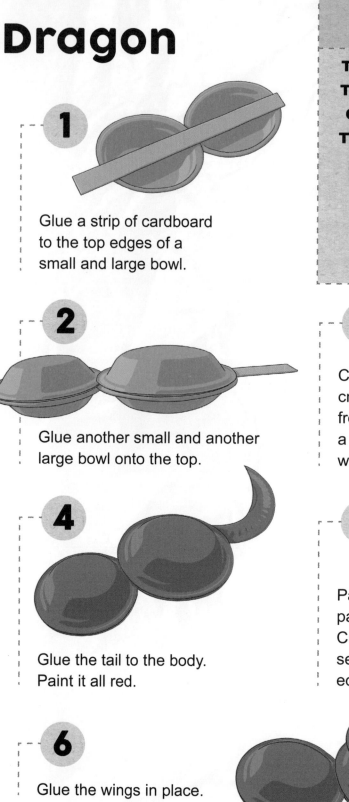 Glue the tail to the body. Paint it all red.

5  Paint a small paper plate red. Cut it in half, then cut out three semicircles along the straight edge of each piece to make wings.

6 Glue the wings in place.

7

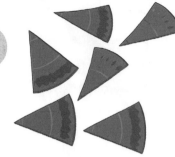

Cut six segments from a small plate and paint red.

8

Glue four segments to the base for feet. Glue two onto the head for crests. Add some details to the wings and body.

9

Glue two bottle tops to the head. Glue the eyes onto the bottle tops. Cut out some teeth from white cardstock and glue them in place. Watch out—your scary dragon is ready to breathe fire!

Handy Hint
If you do not have bottle tops, use pieces of painted cardstock or red felt.

Crown

You will need

One paper plate
Paint, including yellow
Cardstock
Glitter

1 Paint both sides of a paper plate yellow. Use the end of a pencil to make a hole in the center of the plate, then with scissors, cut from the middle to the grooved edge, as shown.

2 Carefully bend the cut sections upward to make a pointed crown.

3 Cut out some circles from cardstock. Paint and add glitter to look like jewels.

4 Glue the jewels to the points on your crown.

5 Add some more detail to the crown and you're ready to rule!

Hot-Air Balloon

1 Paint a bright design onto two plates so they match.

2 Paint a paper bowl brown. Use the end of a pencil to make four evenly spaced holes around the rim. Tie a piece of string in each of the holes.

3 Tape the free ends of the strings to the inside of one of the plates.

4 Glue the other plate to the first plate, trapping the string between them.

5 Glue a loop of ribbon to the top of the balloon so you can hang it up. Now decide which of your lucky toys is going in the basket!

51

Monkey

Love monkeying around?
If you do, you'll have lots of
fun making this mischievous
friend. Just like you, monkeys
love to play!

You will need

One large paper bowl
One small paper bowl
One paper plate
Brown, beige, and
pink paint
Cardboard
Two googly eyes
One bottle top

1

Draw around the paper bowls
onto a piece of cardboard. Add
two circles at the top for ears.
Cut out the shape. Glue the
two bowls to the cardboard.

2

Cut the grooved edge
from a paper plate
for the monkey's
tail. Paint brown.

3

Paint the
monkey's body.
Give it brown
fur and a beige
face and tummy.
Paint the middle
of the ears pink.

4

Use the cardboard to cut
out a pair of legs and arms.
Paint to match the body.

5

Glue the tail, arms, and legs to the back of the body.

Handy Hint

Never throw away leftover cardstock. Keep it for projects, or if it cannot be used, recycle it.

6

Paint on a smile and glue on a pair of googly eyes and a bottle top nose. Your monkey is ready to play!

Piglet

Oink, oink! This curly-tailed piglet is so adorable that you'll want to make a whole litter!

1

Glue the two paper bowls together. Paint the bowls and the plate pink.

2

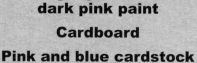

Glue the bowls to the plate.

3

Cut out a pair of ears and feet from the cardboard. Paint them pink.

4

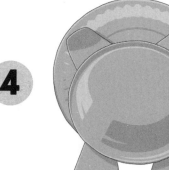

Glue the ears and the feet to the body.

5

Paint the inside of the ears, a snout, and some toenails in darker pink.

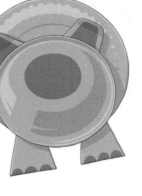

6

Cut out a thin strip of pink cardstock, and wrap it around a pencil, to make a curly tail.

7

Glue the tail in place. Cut out some circles of blue cardstock (slightly bigger than the googly eyes) and glue the eyes to them. Glue the eyes in place. Put your pig with the chickens from pages 34–35 to complete your farmyard!

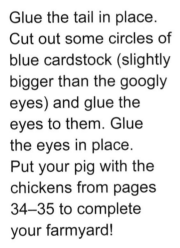

OINK OINK

Angel

This angel is pretty as can be—why not make two or even three!

You will need

One paper plate
One foam ball
Paint
One mini cake case
Two gold foil doilies
One toilet tube
Shiny paper

1

Cut a paper plate in half. Fold one half into a cone (see page 29 for how to do this). Glue into position and paint it a bright color.

2

Paint the foam ball any skin tone. Use the end of a pencil to make a hole in it. Glue the point of the cone into the hole.

3

Add the mini cake case to the head for hair. Draw some features on the face and decorate the cone body with the gold doily.

4

Cut the other half plate in two. These will be the wings. Add some pieces of gold doily to decorate them.

5

Glue the wings to the back of the body.

6

Cut a small ring from a toilet tube and cover with shiny paper, for a halo.

7

Glue the halo in place to complete your angel. She would look lovely on top of a Christmas tree!

Handy Hint
Use glitter paint to add extra details to your pretty angels.

Pirate Beard

You will need

Two paper plates
Black paint
Elastic

1 Cut a paper plate, as shown. The bottom part will be the beard.

2 Cut the edges off another plate for the mustache.

3  Paint the beard and mustache black. Glue the ends of the mustache together.

4 Glue the mustache to the top of the beard.

5 Attach a piece of elastic from one side of the back to the other. Why not make an eye patch, too?

Wiggly Snake

Wiggle, wiggle, wiggle.
This colorful snake
will make you giggle!

You will need

Two paper plates
Paint
Cardboard
Red and blue cardstock
Two googly eyes

1

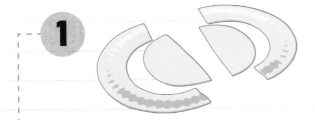

Cut a paper plate in half, cut away the middle sections so you are left with the grooved edges. Repeat this with another plate.

2

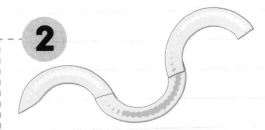

Glue the pieces together, as shown. You can add extra pieces if you want a really long snake. Make the tail pointed.

3

Paint the snake bright colors.

4

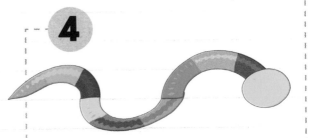

Cut out a large circle of cardboard and paint. Glue to the non-pointed end for the head. Add scaly details.

5

Cut a forked strip of red cardstock for the tongue. Cut out some circles of blue cardstock (slightly bigger than the googly eyes) and glue the eyes to them. Glue these to the head.

Sailboat

You will need

One paper plate
One paper bowl
Red and blue paint
Corrugated cardstock
Cardboard
One straw

1

To make the hull, glue a paper plate to the top of a paper bowl.

2

Paint the hull red. Cut out a circle of corrugated cardstock and glue to the top for the deck.

3

Cut out two triangles from cardboard—one must be slighter bigger than the other. Paint blue to make sails.

4

Glue your sails to a straw, as shown.

5

Make a hole with a pencil in the deck and glue the straw mast in place. Add some more detail to the sails, like stripes and a flag. Now it's time to set sail on the seven seas!

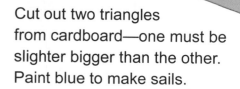

Submarine

1

Glue two paper bowls together and glue the paper cup upside down to the top.

2

Cut out a semicircle from cardboard. Make a slit in the curved side and glue to the rim of the submarine to make the rudder. Paint blue.

3

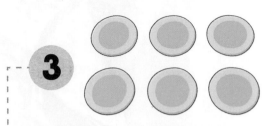

Cut out six circles from cardstock and paint to look like portholes.

4

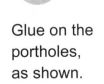

Glue on the portholes, as shown.

5

Make a hole in the top of the submarine with a pencil and push in a piece of bendy straw for the periscope.

6

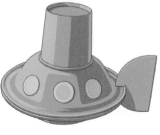

Add some more detail. Your submarine is ready to dive deep into the ocean!

Bunny Mask

Did you know rabbits live in groups? Hop to it and make some bunny masks with your friends!

You will need

One paper plate
Paint
Cardstock
Elastic
Felt, including pink

1 Paint a paper plate whatever color you would like your rabbit to be and fold it in half.

2 Unfold, then make a short slit along the crease. Use the end of a pencil to make holes for your scissors, then cut out two holes for eyes.

3 Cut out a pair of ears from cardstock and paint them to match your rabbit. You could paint the middle of the ears pink.

4  Paint the bottom of the mask a different color. Fold the bottom of the cut end inward so the pieces overlap. Glue into position. Glue on the ears and fold them forward.

5

Attach a piece of elastic from one side of the back to the other.

6

Cut out a felt nose, eyebrows, and some whiskers. Glue them into position. Put on your mask and you are ready to hop, hop, hop away!

Handy Hint

You can add some eyelashes to the bottom of the eyes, too.

Lion Mask

Roar! Put on this fearsome lion mask and become the king of the savannah.

You will need

**One paper plate
Cardstock
Yellow and pink paint
Elastic
Brown and black felt**

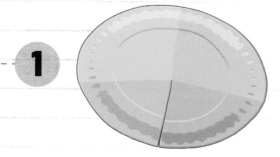

1 Paint a paper plate yellow and fold in half. Unfold and turn over the plate. Make a short slit along the fold line.

2 Use the end of a pencil to make holes for your scissors, then cut out two holes for eyes.

3 Cut out a pair of ears from cardstock. Paint them yellow with a pink middle. Glue them in place.

4 Cut a long strip of brown felt. Cut slits into one edge to make a mane.

5

Glue the mane along the back edge of the plate. Fold the bottom of the cut end inward, so the pieces overlap. Glue into position. Attach a piece of elastic from one side of the back to the other.

6

Cut out a felt nose and some whiskers. Glue them in place. Put on your mask and roar like a lion—did you scare anyone?

ROAR

Snowman

You will need

Two large paper bowls	White, black, and brown paint
Two small paper bowls	Cardboard
One small paper plate	Orange cardstock
	Two googly eyes

1 Glue two large paper bowls together and glue a small bowl to the top. Paint the bowls white.

2 Glue another small bowl to a small plate for the hat. Paint it black.

3 Glue the hat to the head.

4 Cut two twig arms from cardboard and paint them brown.

5 Use the end of a pencil to make holes on either side of the body, slot in the arms and glue into position. Make a small cone nose from a piece of orange cardstock and glue this to the snowman's face.

6 Add a pair of googly eyes and a smile. This friendly snowman will brighten up any winter day!

Cute Cat

You will need

Three paper plates

Light and dark orange paint

Two googly eyes

Green and black felt

1 Cut the grooved edge of a paper plate, as shown.

2 Cut out a small semicircle from the edge of another plate.

3 Glue the cut pieces to a third plate, as shown.

4 Paint your cat orange.

5 Paint on some darker stripes.

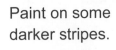

6 Cut out two green felt circles for the eyes and glue to the face. Glue on the googly eyes and a black felt nose. Add a friendly smile and your cat is ready to play!

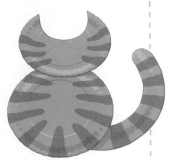

Giraffe

Add some more savannah friends to your collection by making this gorgeous giraffe.

You will need

One small paper plate
One paper bowl
Yellow, brown, pink, and green paint
Cardboard
Brown corrugated cardstock
One googly eye

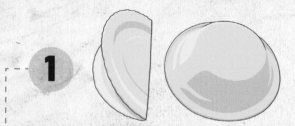

1 Fold a small paper plate in half. This will be the head. Paint the plate and the bowl yellow.

2 Cut out three long strips of cardboard and paint yellow for the legs and neck.

3 From cardboard, cut out a circle the same size as the bowl. Glue the legs and neck to the circle.

4 Glue the bowl onto the circle of cardstock, and the head to the neck.

5 Paint on lots of brown spots.

6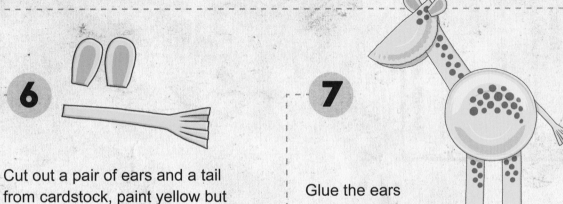

Cut out a pair of ears and a tail from cardstock, paint yellow but make the middle of the ears pink. Give the tail a fringed end.

7

Glue the ears and tail in place.

Handy Hint

If you do not have corrugated cardstock for the mane, cut tiny slits into plain cardstock.

8

Cut out a circle, paint it green, and attach the googly eye to it. Glue the circle in place. Cut some strips of brown cardstock for the mane and hooves. Glue to the body. Add a nose and a smile. Your giraffe is ready for the savannah!

Polly Parrot

**Who's a pretty parrot?
This colorful crafty friend!**

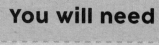

1 Paint a paper plate red and fold in half.

2 Cut out a beak from cardboard and paint black.

3 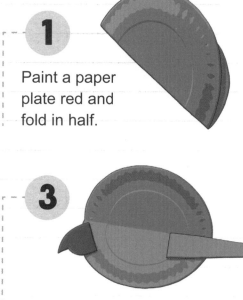 Cut a tail from cardboard and paint red. Glue the beak and tail to the inside edges of the plate. Fold the plate, trapping the tail and beak inside. Glue in place.

4  Cut out a pair of wings from another plate and paint with a red, yellow, and blue stripe.

5 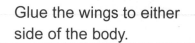 Glue the wings to either side of the body.

6

Cut out two circles from white cardstock and glue to either side of the head. Cut smaller green circles of cardstock, glue on the eyes, then glue in place.

7

Use the end of a pencil to make a hole for your scissors, then cut out the middle from another plate. Paint this grooved ring brown.

8

Cut a slit into both sides of the parrot's body at the bottom.

CAW
CAW

9

Slide the parrot onto the inside of the ring and glue to hold in place. Add a loop of ribbon to the top of the ring so you can hang it up. Watch it sway to and fro, just like a real parrot!

Barking Dog Hand Puppet

Woof, woof, woof! Make this noisy puppet pal and entertain all your friends with its bark.

1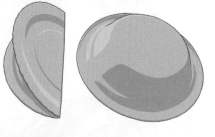

Fold the plate in half, paint it pink on the inside and light brown on the outside.
Paint the bowl light brown.

2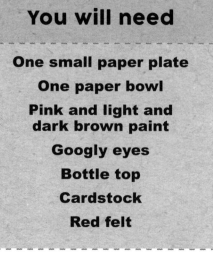

Glue half of the brown side of the plate to the top of the bowl.

3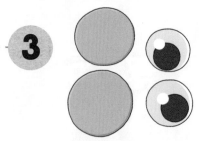

Cut out some circles of cardstock (slightly bigger than the googly eyes) and paint the circles brown. Glue on the googly eyes. Fold back the bottom of the eye circle, to make a flat edge.

4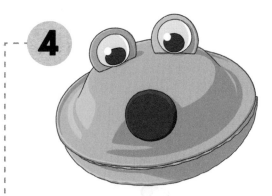

Add glue to the underside of the folded piece and glue the eyes to the head, as shown. Add a bottle top for the nose.

5

Cut out a pair of ears from cardstock and paint them dark brown.

6

Fold the bottom of the ears back and glue in place.

7

Cut out a tongue from red felt.

8

Glue the tongue inside the mouth and paint some spots on the head. Place your fingers into the bowl and your thumb under the mouth—now make your dog bark!

WOOF
WOOF

Nest of Chicks

These little chicks are so sweet! Why not make a nestful?

You will need

One paper bowl

Light brown and orange cardstock

Six googly eyes

Yellow and brown paint

Two paper plates

Three foam balls

1

Paint a paper bowl brown. Cut some narrow strips of light brown cardstock and glue to the bowl to look like twigs.

2

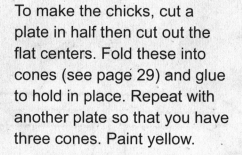

To make the chicks, cut a plate in half then cut out the flat centers. Fold these into cones (see page 29) and glue to hold in place. Repeat with another plate so that you have three cones. Paint yellow.

3

Use a pencil to make a large hole in each foam ball, glue one to the top of each cone. Paint the balls yellow.

4

Cut six sections from the edge of the plate and paint yellow to make wings for each chick.

5

Fold the bottom of the wings and glue the wings to the bodies.

6

Add some orange cardstock beaks and googly eyes. Carefully place your chicks in their nest.

CHEEP
CHEEP

Mother Duck

Five little ducklings went swimming one day. Quack, quack! It's time for mother duck to bring them home.

1

Cut the large paper plate, as shown.

2

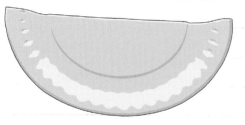

Cut the other large plate in half. Glue one half to the back of the first plate so that the duck can stand.

3

Paint your plates brown, green, and white to look like a duck.

Handy Hint

Ducks come in all colors—why not make a few?

76

4

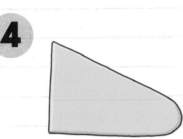

Cut out a beak from cardboard and paint yellow.

5

Glue the beak and a googly eye in place.

6

Repeat steps 1 to 5 with smaller plates to make five yellow ducklings. Line them up in a row!

QUACK

Santa

It's Christmastime! You'll have lots of fun making this jolly Santa—ho, ho, ho!

You will need

Three large paper plates

One small paper plate

Red and white paint

Black and yellow cardstock

Red pompom

Two googly eyes

1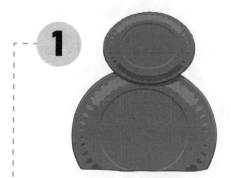

Cut off the bottom of a large plate. Glue a small plate to the top. Paint both red.

2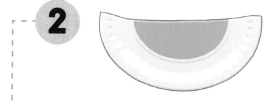

Cut another large plate in half. Paint the middle to make Santa's face.

3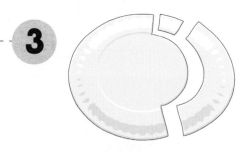

Cut the grooved edge off another large plate, as shown. This will be the fur trim on the hat.

4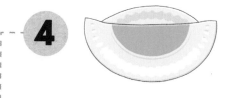

Glue the long piece of fur trim to the top of the face.

5

Glue the head to the body.

6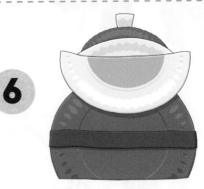

Add a black strip of cardstock for the belt. Add the small piece of fur trim to the hat.

7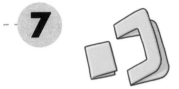

Cut out a buckle from yellow cardstock and glue to the belt.

8

Cut out a mustache from the edge of the small plate.

9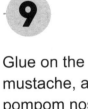

Glue on the mustache, a pompom nose, and some googly eyes. Ho, ho, ho, your Santa is ready to go!

Quarto is the authority on a wide range of topics.

Quarto educates, entertains and enriches the lives of our readers—enthusiasts and lovers of hands-on living.

www.quartoknows.com

Design and Editorial: Calcium
Photography: Michael Wicks
Illustration: Tom Connell
With thanks to our wonderful models Islah, Ethan and Ania.

First published in the United States in 2016
by QEB Publishing, Inc.
Part of The Quarto Group
6 Orchard
Lake Forest, CA 92630

A CIP record for this book is available from the Library of Congress.

ISBN 978 1 68297 006 5

Printed in China